6/77

```
j974.8   Lengyel, Emil, 1895-              77 28
Le          The Colony of Pennsylvania.  New
         York, Watts, 1974.
            86 p.  illus.  23 cm.

            Bibliography:  p. 81-82.




                  1. Pennsylvania - History.
           I. Title.
   POCK CARD     770425
   7579109                    SF      Ortega Branch
```

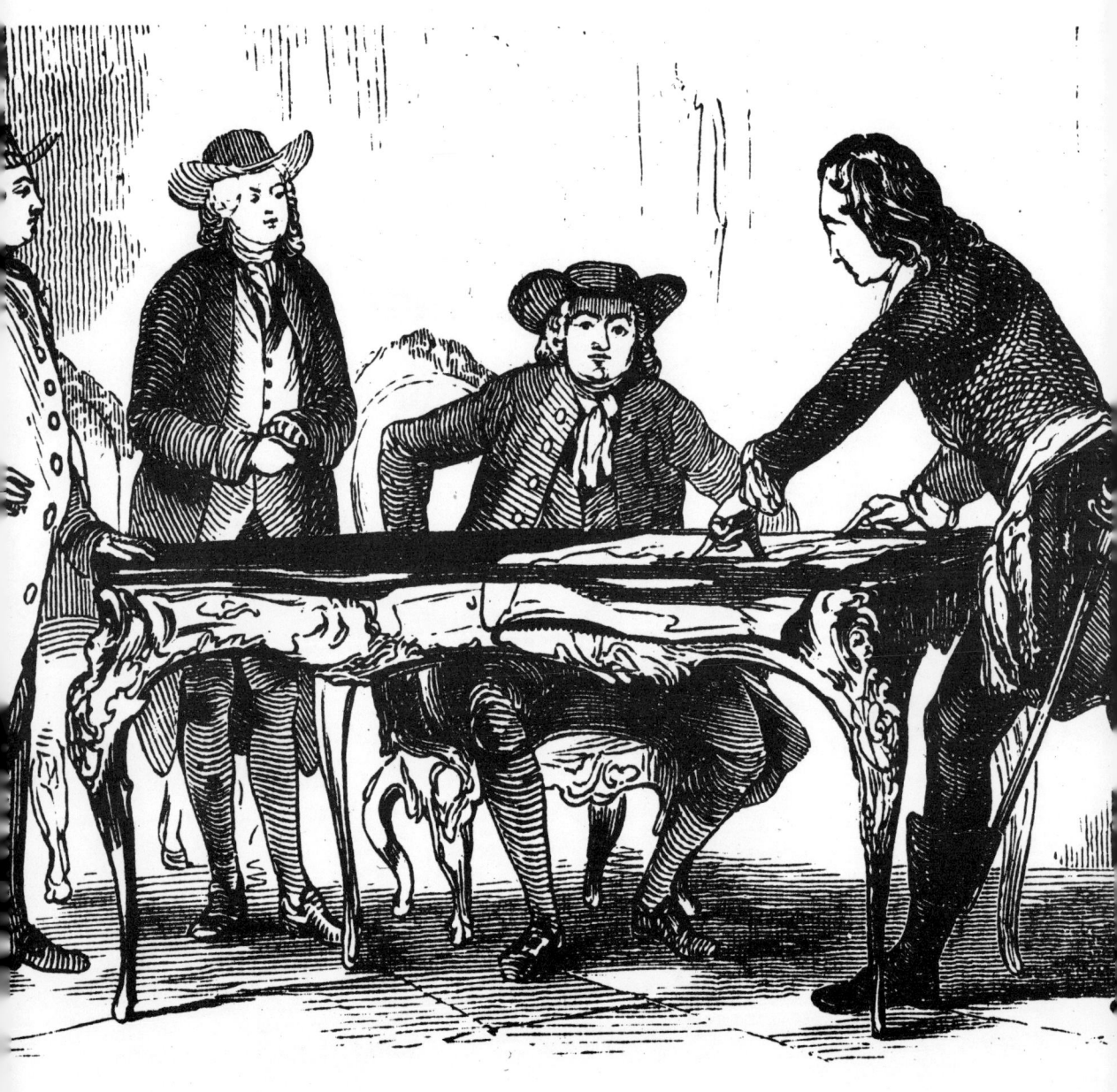

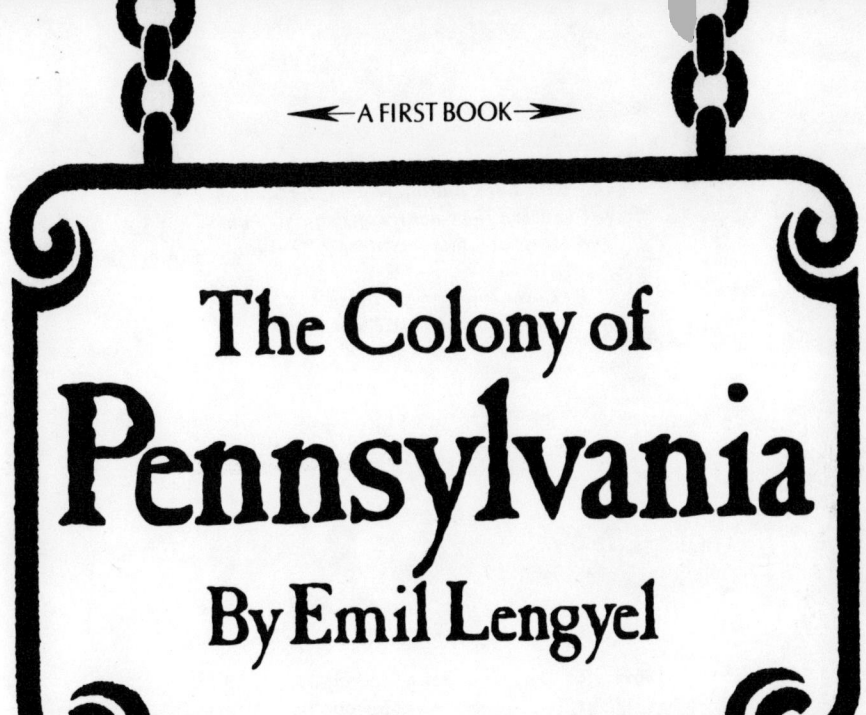

←A FIRST BOOK→

The Colony of Pennsylvania
By Emil Lengyel

ILLUSTRATED WITH
CONTEMPORARY PRINTS
AND PHOTOGRAPHS

FRANKLIN WATTS | NEW YORK | LONDON

Title page photograph shows William Penn (seated) arguing with Lord Baltimore over the boundary line between the colonies of Pennsylvania and Maryland, late seventeenth century.

Cover photograph shows the colony's founder, William Penn.

Photographs courtesy of:

Library of Congress: pp. 9, 15, 18, 23, 25, 28, 34, 42–43, 51, 52, 59, 69, 70; Metropolitan Museum of Art: p. 74; New York Public Library Picture Collection: title page, pp. 2, 10, 32, 37, 60, 63; New York Public Library Spencer Collection: p. 46.

Library of Congress Cataloging in Publication Data

Lengyel, Emil
    The Colony of Pennsylvania.

    (A First book)
    SUMMARY: A history of the tenth colony founded in America, which became known as the Keystone State.
    Bibliography: p.
    1. Pennsylvania–History–Colonial period–Juvenile literature. 2. Pennsylvania–History–Revolution–Juvenile literature. [1. Pennsylvania–History–Colonial Period] I. Title.
F152.L54   917.48′03′2   74-846
ISBN 0-531-02721-X

Copyright © 1974 by Franklin Watts, Inc.
Printed in the United States of America
6 5 4 3

Introduction
1

A Reckless Explorer
4

The Road to "India"
6

William Penn and History
12

A Land of Sylvan Beauty
27

The City of Brotherly Love
39

The Quakers and the Indians
48

Trouble in England and the Colony
56

Franklin and the Revolution
62

The Way to Statehood
72

Important Dates in Colonial Pennsylvania
77

Some Colonial Sights in Modern Pennsylvania
79

For Further Reading
81

Index
83

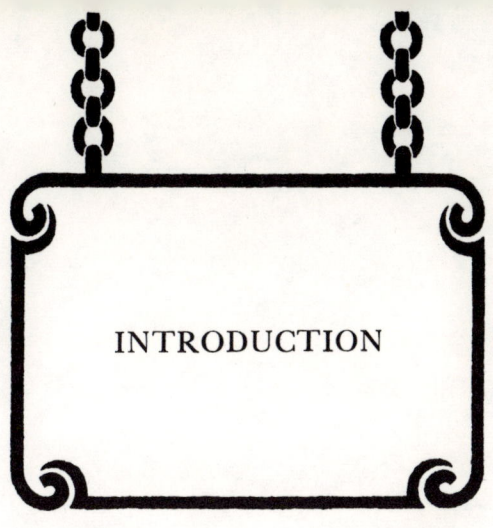

INTRODUCTION

Pennsylvania's nickname is the Keystone State. In colonial times, Pennsylvania was the keystone of the British colonies because of its pivotal place between its neighbors to the north and south. The commonwealth is equally proud of its motto—"Virtue, Liberty, and Independence." Colonial Pennsylvania's hospitality to all creeds was a sign of its "virtue." It proclaimed "liberty" when the Declaration of Independence was framed in the colony's largest city, Philadelphia, called the City of Brotherly Love. Pennsylvania created the framework of the "independence" of the United States by playing a key role in developing the Constitution. Even after the proclamation of independence, Pennsylvania continued to play a leading role —as a keystone of America's economic development and the first major center of its growing industries. Eventually, it became the most important industrial state of the new country.

Pennsylvania was the tenth of the original thirteen colo-

*A boundary stone marking the Mason and Dixon line,
separating Pennsylvania and Maryland.
The stones were set up a mile apart;
every fifth one showing the arms of Penn on one side
and the arms of Lord Baltimore on the other.*

nies, its charter dating from 1681. One of four states to be called a commonwealth (Kentucky, Massachusetts, and Virginia are the others), Pennsylvania became the second state of the new United States of America in 1787. It was named for its founder's father, Admiral William Penn. In size, it ranks thirty-third of the fifty states, with an area of 45,333 square miles.

The Commonwealth of Pennsylvania, with its capital at Harrisburg, is one of the Middle Atlantic states. It is bounded on the east by New Jersey and New York (separated by the Delaware River); on the north by New York and Lake Erie; on the west by West Virginia and Ohio; and on the south by West Virginia, Maryland, and Delaware. Except for the small boundary with Delaware, Pennsylvania's southern border is the famous Mason and Dixon Line. Originally fixed to settle a boundary dispute between Pennsylvania and Maryland, the Mason and Dixon Line became the divider between North and South, with Pennsylvania in its keystone position.

A RECKLESS EXPLORER

Unlike its northern neighbors (New Jersey, New York, and the New England colonies) and the southern colonies all the way to Georgia, the colony of Pennsylvania did not face directly on the Atlantic Ocean. It was hidden in its lush, wooded mountain ranges. In the other colonies, explorers came from the sea, but probably the first white man to set eyes on Pennsylvania came through the back door, so to speak. He was an adventurous young Frenchman, Étienne Brulé (c. 1592–1632). Born in Paris, Brulé was still a boy when he joined (in 1608) the exploring and fur-trading team of his fellow countryman, Samuel de Champlain, whose base was in Canada where he founded the city of Quebec.

The wily Champlain recognized the bold and adventurous traits of young Étienne. He induced the boy to learn Indian language and woodcraft by joining the tribe of Iroqet, the Algonquian chief. When Brulé was twenty, the restless young man joined the Hurons (whose name means "ruffian"). Huron tribesmen were great wanderers, and Brulé was attracted to them because of his desire to see unknown lands. When he returned to the French camp, he served as Champlain's interpreter, and was soon dispatched on a new mission to the Conestoga. (Their name means "Place of Muddy Water," which was the Upper Susquehanna River, the main encampment.) With them Brulé cut straight across the center of Pennsylvania. He descended the Susquehanna River all the way to Chesapeake Bay.

Brulé returned north after this exploration to live with the Hurons, whom he seems to have preferred among all the tribes. But in 1632, during a drunken brawl, he went on a rampage, and his Indian companions killed and ate him. The Hurons practiced cannibalism, particularly after killing a brave enemy. By consuming his heart, they hoped to acquire his courage. In a way, it might be said that the Hurons paid Brulé a "compliment."

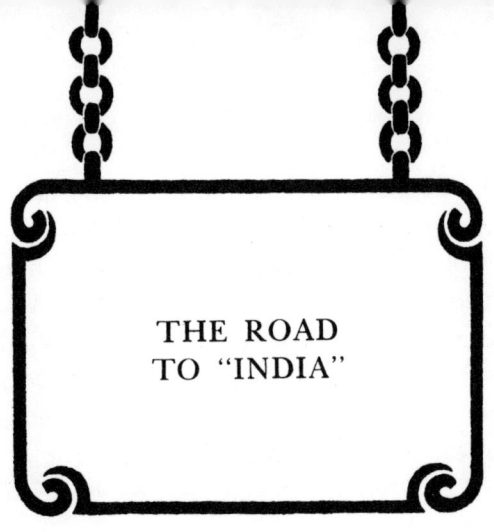

THE ROAD TO "INDIA"

In the fifteenth century, as before and since, daring explorers were eager to face the unknown. India and China were two lands that much attracted them. They wanted the highly valued silk, spices, and gems from those regions. Columbus, as we know, called the original inhabitants of the Americas "Indians," because he thought he had found the outlying regions of the large Indian subcontinent. Other explorers wanted to reach China by finding a Northwest Passage across the American continent.

Several explorers became familiar with what is now Panama in Central America, where the narrowest point between the Atlantic and Pacific oceans measures about thirty miles. They thought that much the same situation would exist in North America. They hoped to cross a narrow tongue of land and find themselves on the Pacific coast. From there they could easily sail to China and India. They could not have known, of course, that the American continent was no few miles wide, but some three thousand miles from coast to coast. And the distance between the westernmost coast of North America and the easternmost shoreline of Asia is at least twice that long. But because they had no way of knowing those facts they kept on trying, imitating Columbus's "splendid mistake."

The boldest explorers in North America represented some of the smallest countries of northern Europe. Poor in natural resources, they were impressed by the wealth of the Far East. The first explorers in what became Pennsylvania, and the adjacent regions, were the Dutch, the Swedes, and the British.

Henry Hudson was an Englishman in the service of the Dutch. In the early seventeenth century he set out to find a passage to the Far East. He first tried the Delaware River, today's boundary between Pennsylvania and its eastern neighbors; next (in 1609) the river that now bears his name. Sailing up the Hudson in the hope of reaching China, he got as far as today's Albany, New York. It was Hudson's voyages that gave the Netherlands its claim to the central region of the Atlantic coast. For all Hudson's pains, however, he had a tragic end. The crews of his ships, not as courageous as he, mutinied and set him, his son, and a few others adrift in a small boat without food and water. They were never seen again.

The Dutch established themselves in the heartland of the future mid-Atlantic colonies. Peter Minuit, director-general (1626–31) of the colony of New Netherland, transacted one of history's best real estate sales. He bought the island of Manhattan (site of New York City) for trinkets worth about sixty Dutch guilders, or some $24. When he was later dismissed from the service of the Dutch, he was employed by the Swedish chancellor, Axel Oxenstierna, to found a settlement in the heartland of the North Atlantic coast.

The settlement that Minuit created for the Swedes included parts of eastern Pennsylvania, New Jersey, and Delaware, where he acquired land from the Indians. (He also engaged in a highly profitable fur trade.) Minuit named the country New Sweden. For its protection he had Fort Christina (now Wilmington, Delaware) built on the Delaware River. About half of the Swedish colonists were Finns, since Finnish lands in Europe were then part of Sweden. Because of the abundance of wood in the region, the settlers built log cabins, and they became the models for the log dwellings of the American frontier. As for Peter Minuit, he shared the fate of many adventurers; he was lost at sea in 1638.

In 1646 the Dutch appointed Peter Stuyvesant director-general of New Netherland and adjacent regions. As a swashbuckling soldier in the Dutch army, he had lost his right leg in a campaign in Central American waters.

Stuyvesant was an efficient administrator and commander. He drove the Swedes out of New Sweden in 1655, and extended Dutch territory into Pennsylvania. The economic conditions of the region improved under his rule. But Stuyvesant had no patience with critics, was intolerant of political opposition, and acted much like a dictator.

The Dutchman, for all his faults, may have been an excellent soldier, but his country could not match the naval power of the British, who wanted the Dutch-held territory. Stuyvesant was forced to surrender to the British on September 4, 1664. Although the Dutch would regain the area from July, 1673 to August, 1674, a new chapter in the history of this region of North America had begun.

The British were already in power in Virginia, where they had established a foothold at Jamestown in 1607. In New England the settlement of Plymouth was started by passengers

Peter Minuit trading for land with native Americans

An early Swedish church in the New World

from the *Mayflower* in 1620. Now the British added New Netherland to their possessions. And Charles II, then on the throne of England, transferred possession of the land to his brother, the Duke of York (later James II).

Little was known about most of the new area the British held, especially the part that became Pennsylvania. It was a heavily wooded region ("sylvan"—Penn*sylvan*ia—means wooded in Latin), filled with mountains, hills, and streams.

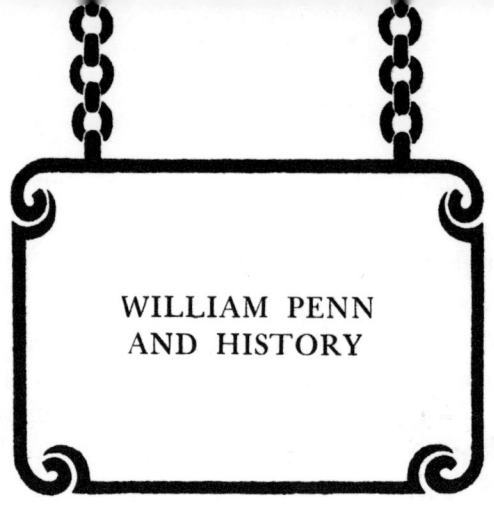

WILLIAM PENN AND HISTORY

At the age of twenty-eight, Sir William Penn, father of the founder of Pennsylvania, was already a noted admiral in the service of Great Britain. A man of willpower and more than average intelligence, endowed with great self-confidence and a commanding personality, he held some of the highest offices of seventeenth-century England, a turbulent country in a turbulent age. Admiral Penn fought and scored victories against the Spaniards and the Dutch. Therefore, many honors and such grandiose titles as Great Captain Commander were his. Penn also served under the Duke of York, who had respect and admiration for him.

The Admiral's son, William Junior (1644–1718), was endowed with all the advantages to be given a child of a famous father. Young William had a pleasant face, regular features, friendly eyes, and a good mind. At eleven years old he voiced opinions about matters more generally reserved for learned men.

At the age of sixteen, William entered Christ Church College of Oxford University. We can judge his critical mind from his criticism of Oxford, which was (and still is) considered one of the best universities in the world. He denounced it and other English universities, with which he seems to have had some contact, as "signal places of idleness, looseness, profaneness, prodigality, and gross ignorance." (He was expelled for religious nonconformity in 1662.)

The turbulence of that age had extended to matters of religion. Indeed, the turbulence was strongest concerning one's faith. The Church of England had been created in a split from the Roman Catholic Church during the reign of Henry VIII (1509–47). Now the king of England was head not only of the state but also of the church. While the official church in England was gaining strength, Catholic opposition was still strong. With the religious split had come a time of questioning. What was the Christian to believe? On the continent, Protestantism resulted in the creation of numerous sects, all of which claimed to represent the Divine Will. Questions about religious beliefs were also asked in England, and there, too, a number of sects arose.

In his teens young William Penn asked questions about religion that children of the higher classes were not supposed to ask. This independence of mind angered his father, whose friend, the Duke of York, was a believer in the Catholic creed. But young Penn believed that religion was a matter of individual conscience. He believed in Christian values and he believed in God and Christ. But he wanted to believe in them in his own way. Every person, he thought, was a unique creation and could not be expected to march in lockstep. Indeed, young Penn went so far as to assert that man could communicate with God directly and that the mediation of the clergy was unnecessary.

About 1657 Penn had first heard the teachings of the religious leader, George Fox (1624–91), who founded what he first called Friends of Truth, and then the Society of Friends. Members of the society were to live a life of truth. They would find such a life by looking into themselves, seeking to discover their real natures, being guided by the "inner light" which reveals the truth. In the society, religion was a full-time, not a part-time, concern. One lived a moral life until death. No clergy were needed for the individual to find him or herself. Nor was a church needed, because the House of Truth was everywhere. Doctrines and dogmas were unnecessary; they sought to force a common pattern on a unique lifetime's traits and experiences.

The Society of Friends soon gained the name of Quakers, because they were said to "quake in the presence of God" while comparing their imperfections with His perfection. The Quakers considered each other friends, called each other by first names, and when addressing one another they dropped the formal "you" in favor of the informal "thee" and "thou." This feeling of friendship was eventually extended to all people.

The Friends had meeting places, not to follow a ritual but to be inspired by each other's presence. They looked into themselves, seeking communion with a higher reality. Suddenly, the inner light would show what they were seeking. Then one Friend might want to stand up and speak to his fellow Quakers, sharing his spiritual experience with them. To the Quakers, the Bible was a lofty book to be read and reread, but it was not the unfailing guide that it was to the Puritans in New England.

Quakers in a meetinghouse

William Penn became a Quaker in 1667 (for which his father threatened to—but did not—disinherit him). The Quakers were distrusted in the England of the time. Since loyalty was not only to one's country, but also to the official church, members of special sects were considered subversives and perhaps foes of the monarch. And, of course, Quaker teachings were a protest against the Church of England.

From his conversion until 1669, Penn spent some time in the Tower of London, imprisoned largely because of his books concerning his religious beliefs. After one of his imprisonments, he was told he could go free if he returned to the official church. "My prison shall be my grave before I budge a jot," he is said to have replied, "for I owe my conscience to no mortal man."

Penn was a strong missionary of the Quaker creed. To reach larger audiences, he wrote leaflets, pamphlets, tracts, and books. *Truth Exalted* (1668) upheld the simplicity of the Quaker message. *The Sandy Foundation Shaken* (1668) attacked the Trinity. His greatest book, *No Cross, No Crown* (1669), assailed the unchristian lives of some clergymen and the Church of England itself.

In 1670, now twenty-six years old, Penn was headed one day for the Quaker meetinghouse on Gracechurch Street, London. When he and other Friends arrived, they found the door padlocked. The police had heard of the proposed meeting and had acted in accordance with the order of the authorities.

The Quakers were law-abiding, but they drew a line between law and tyranny. To William Penn particularly, this action violated an Englishman's rights. At the same time, the Quakers held the belief that one did not need an enclosed meeting place to exalt God and to relate one's experiences in search of truth. So Penn began to speak to his fellow Quakers in the street. The authorities promptly arrested him for "inciting to a riot" and marched him once more off to jail.

In September of that year, Penn was placed on trial with other Quakers. Perhaps because of his distinguished family or the importance of the case, the mayor of the borough and his recorder were also present. Nominally, the case was in the hands of a jury, whose foreman was named Edward Bushell. He, the other members of the jury, the mayor, the recorder, and the judge were communicants in the Church of England. Together with most of their countrymen, they held the view that only a loyal Anglican could be loyal to the king.

Because of his ability, William Penn, the youngest defendant, was asked by the other accused to speak for them all. He might have argued that they were all loyal to the king, despite the fact that everyone knew Charles II was hardly a moral character himself. Penn, who had access to the court through his father, knew, for instance, that the head of the Anglican Church (the king) had countless mistresses, among them the well-known actress Nell Gwynn. He also might have told the jury that he and the others could not incite riots because the Quakers were people of peace who did not believe in violence of any kind.

Instead, Penn spoke about the Quakers' creed, of their hatred of violence and their attachment to the laws of God and the just laws of man. He told the jury that the Friends not only avoided violence, but that they believed in the scriptural word about "turning the other cheek." However, they also believed in God's law to follow their own consciences.

Although all the jurors were Church of England men who thoroughly disagreed with the religious views of Penn and his fellow prisoners, they were deeply convinced by Penn's words. Accordingly, they brought in a verdict of not guilty.

The anger of the judge, the mayor, and the recorder at the verdict was so intense that they took an unusual step, even for the times. They had Bushell and the other jurors fined for violation of the legal code and imprisoned. Later, however, Sir John Vaughan, the Lord Chief Justice, made the declaration that a "judge may try to open the jurors' eyes, but not to lead them by the nose." This asserted for all time the independence of the jury, and represents a landmark in English law.

To spread the teachings of the Quakers, in the 1670s Penn wrote about forty tracts, and also visited Holland, some of the German lands, Switzerland, and Russia. The faith of the Quakers was spreading there, too. In western Germany (at the time Germany was not one nation, but a number of independent states), in an area known as the Palatinate, Penn converted Princess Elizabeth, the granddaughter of James I, to his creed. Some of her subjects followed her.

In the Germanies, Penn became acquainted with religious sects holding much in common with the Friends. Among these were many who later followed him to America, where their descendants still constitute well-known religious groups. The Mennonites were probably the best known, named after their founder, Meno Simons. Like the Quakers, they rejected participation in wars and stood for nonresistance. They rejected oath-taking, practiced adult baptism, wanted only loose relations with the state, and restricted marriages to members of the group. From the Mennonites grew the Amish Church, named for Jacob Amen. They form a small and picturesque religious group in Pennsylvania even today. The Hutterian Brethren, named after Jacob Hutter, not only shared the paci-

William Penn, founder of the colony of Pennsylvania

fist and nonresistance features of the creed of the Friends, but were also opposed to private property. Their lands were held by the community for the use of the entire religious sect.

Penn was also successful in spreading his faith in his own family circle. In 1672, two years after his father's death (he inherited his father's estates in England and Ireland), Penn married a woman of great beauty and intelligence, Gulielma Maria Springett. Under her husband's influence, she left the Anglican Church to join the Quakers. They had eight children, only four surviving infancy.

In a country where religious conformity was a test of loyalty, the Quakers of England fell on hard times. They were persecuted, kept from filling important public offices, and many were even imprisoned. Subsequently some of them were released, since the government under King Charles was at best whimsical, and often operated in a haphazard way. And in the North American territories, their lot was not much better. In New England, with the exception of Rhode Island, the Puritans ruled. Victims of persecution in their native England, many of them became persecutors overseas. The New England Quakers were among their victims.

Penn became involved in the colonial scene in a somewhat roundabout way. Sir George Carteret, one-time governor of the English Channel island of Jersey, and Lord John Berkeley had received a grant of land from the Duke of York, which came to be called New Jersey. Part of the land was later bought by two Quakers—John Fenwick, sometime major in the Parliamentary army during the English Civil War, and Edward Byllynge, a prominent merchant. As members of the Society of Friends, they should have been personal friends, too, but they were not. They quarreled between themselves and after a business dispute, they needed an arbitrator. They asked William Penn to serve in that capacity. For his pains he received a share of the property. Under his influence, the owners drew up the "Concessions and Agreements" (1676) of West New Jersey, a remarkable document providing for religious freedom and the election of judges and members of the assembly. Trials were to be by jury, and elections by ballot. Each member of the assembly would receive a small compensation to show that he was not the master, but the servant, of the people. These were very democratic practices for the time.

Slowly an idea was taking root in Penn's mind. The Quakers and many other sects were persecuted in England, as the Hebrews had been in the ancient Egypt of the Pharaohs. When their lot had become intolerable, the Hebrews left Egypt to go to Canaan, the Promised Land. Maybe there was such a Promised Land in North America. In the New World there could be a new beginning, for ancient traditions would not weigh upon the people, and Penn knew that tradition was often related to oppression. In that sylvan land, all people could be treated as equal, whatever their birth or creed. Perhaps in America such a dream might succeed. Penn called the idea a "holy experiment," and he thought of a way to make the idea a reality.

From 1660 until 1685 Charles II, of the House of Stuart and known as the "Merry Monarch," sat on the throne of England. Charles I, his father, had been beheaded, the loser in his fight for power with the British Parliament. The first Charles had led a life of danger for eleven years, in hiding for a time and then again in exile. Those years of British history became known as the Commonwealth period, the reign of the Lord Protector, Oliver Cromwell. Commonwealth rule ended in 1660 when Charles II, then thirty years old, was proclaimed king. Unlike his father, he had submitted to the terms demanded by Parliament.

Admiral William Penn had acted carefully during these troubled times. Officially on the side of the ruling Parliament, he still maintained close contact with the royalists. Actually, he did more than that. A man of wealth, he loaned money to the royal Court, about £16,000 (equal at the time to $60,000). Sometime after his father's death, young William Penn proposed a way in which the king could repay that debt. The king's brother, the Duke of York, now held enormously large estates in America, reaching deep inland on the mid-Atlantic coast. In repayment of the loan, Penn wanted a large tract of land from the Duke's holdings.

British America was royal property. The king (or queen) could dispose of it in several ways. He (or she) might want to retain it under royal control, or grant charters to trading companies overseas: the Virginia Company, the Plymouth Company, and the Hudson Bay Company, among others. These were private corporations under royal control, with most of the power in the company directors' hands. The monarch could create proprietary colonies by granting them to individuals. The proprietors exercised governmental powers, but were subject to royal supervision. Territorial grants to individuals were often called baronies.

Much of the Duke of York's land in the mid-Atlantic region of America had already been assigned to others. But there was a large area, farther inland and with no direct access to the Atlantic Ocean, which was still unassigned. Penn knew about it in a vague way. He had heard that much of it was covered with impenetrable forests—a "sylvan" land. He also knew that in spite of the large extent of the forests, the region had great

Penn receives the charter for Pennsylvania from Charles II.

tracts of farmland in river valleys and on hill slopes. All in all, this seemed like a desirable place for the holy experiment, where his Quakers might live in peace.

King Charles was pleased with Penn's suggestion. He liked it far more than a cash demand for the repayment of money he owed. Besides, Charles did not think much of the value of his overseas domains. Rather, he regarded them as wildernesses filled with savages. However, he wished to play the generous ruler.

"You will see on this paper," he said to Penn, "that I have done something handsome for you. I have given you in North America as large a territory as my own island of Great Britain." But the king believed that he had the better part of the bargain.

William Penn suggested that the territory be called New Wales, for the original location of the Penn family. But Charles wanted to commemorate the name of his late friend, Admiral William Penn. The name of the colony, he said, was to be Pennsylvania—Penn in memory of his friend; sylvania because it was heavily wooded. But the name could be misunderstood, the younger Penn argued. The world might think that he had named the colony for himself. Charles, however, stuck to his decision; the grant was to be called Pennsylvania. It was a proprietary colony in which the proprietor could act almost as if he were the king. Penn comforted himself half jokingly that the name of his grant was not really that bad. His last name meant "high" in the Welsh language. Pennsylvania, in a mixture of Welsh and Latin, meant, therefore, "high woodlands." And that it was, indeed.

Penn leaves England for his first look at his "holy experiment."

Penn's grant in 1681 extended some 300 miles east to west and about 160 miles north to south, approximately the dimensions of the modern state. (Some boundary disputes had to be settled through the years to reach the state lines of Pennsylvania today. The most famous was the dispute with Maryland over Pennsylvania's southern border, finally settled in 1767 by two prominent English surveyors, Charles Mason and Jeremiah Dixon. An agreement with Virginia, which at one time claimed the upper Ohio Valley, extended the Mason and Dixon Line so that Lake Erie became part of Pennsylvania's western boundary. Connecticut claimed part of northeastern Pennsylvania—the two actually got into physical conflict about it in what are known as the Pennamite Wars. A congressional commission decided in favor of Pennsylvania near the end of the American Revolution. Pennsylvania and New York settled their boundary dispute in 1789, agreeing on the 42nd parallel as Pennsylvania's northern boundary. If extended to Lake Erie, the line would have left Pennsylvania with very little lake front, so arrangements were made to buy the Lake Erie triangle, now a part of Pennsylvania.)

In 1681, the stage had just been set to carry out William Penn's holy experiment. Accordingly, in September of the following year, he left England on the sailing boat *Welcome* for the "land of sylvan beauty."

A LAND OF SYLVAN BEAUTY

The two proprietors of New Jersey, Berkeley and Carteret, had written enthusiastically to Penn about the beauty and wealth of the land which was to be his across the Delaware River. They described Pennsylvania as a land where the mighty forests rose, tall and stately, darkening the western sky with their blue shade and stretching north and south along the river as far as the astonished eye could travel.

The mountains which they called "blue" are now known as the Red Mountains. But in haze they do appear to be blue. Their redness is caused by iron in their limestone, sandstone, and shale. Pennsylvania is not only wooded, but also mountainous. It is cut by the Appalachian Range, extending far beyond the state boundaries to Canada on the one side and to Alabama on the other.

Colonial Pennsylvania was not only beautiful, but also rich in natural resources. It came to be called the "larder" by

This early engraving shows some of Pennsylvania's hills and woodlands.

some, due to its wealth in game. Rabbits and partridges were numerous, and wild turkeys were in such abundance that the tree branches on which they perched seemed to be black with them. The New Jersey proprietors had written about Pennsylvania's animal life, too: "Walking through the woods, we were ever and anon starting up the deer in droves and were frequently within sight of large herds of buffalo, wallowing in fat and seeming in their course to shake the earth with their weight."

Penn's colony had endless stands of timber, virgin forests of oaks and elms and many other valuable trees. Here was ample material for the frontiersmen's dwellings, household articles, and farmers' tools. Indian trails wound through the thick forests, linking with others in the adjacent colonies.

The soil of Pennsylvania along its water courses was a black mold, deep and rich where the Indian corn grew to an "enormous size." Penn's land was also abounding in rivers and waterways, which aided transportation across the heavily wooded land and provided rich hauls of fish. The easternmost portion of the colony depended largely on the frontier river, the Delaware, and its main tributaries, the Schuylkill ("hidden river" in Dutch) and the Lehigh, another stream of great natural beauty.

Cutting straight across Pennsylvania, settlers found the Susquehanna, an Indian name meaning "muddy stream." In the western part of the colony were other widespread river systems, especially the Monongahela (an Indian word meaning "stream with the sliding banks") and the Allegheny. These two form the Ohio River, nearly 1,000 miles long, a major tributary of the Mississippi and Pennsylvania's link to the West.

While the forests were the colony's hunting grounds, its many streams were the fisherman's paradise. The Delaware was so full of sturgeon that observers had to wait barely a minute to see one of these great fishes leaping from the water into the air, "not without much fright," according to the account, "to the natives whose canoes they have many a time fallen into and overset." Great also was the number of wild geese and ducks.

However, the early colonists did not see the real wealth of Pennsylvania because much of it was underground. It was only later that the settlers made the discoveries of great natural resources. On a mere 500 square miles in the east-central portion of Pennsylvania, much of this country's vast hard coal (anthracite) deposits are concentrated. Pennsylvania is also rich in soft (bituminous) coal.

King Charles II was surely mistaken when he thought he had gained the better part of the bargain in charging $60,000 for this land of nearly inexhaustible wealth.

Penn's proprietary rights in this new colony were broad, and he was relatively free to build his ideal community. To make it more ideal, he obtained from the Duke of York an access to the sea by way of the Delaware River. "I have led the greatest colony into America," he commented, "that ever man did upon a private credit, and the most prosperous beginnings that were ever in it are to be found among us."

Penn wanted his colony to prosper spiritually as well. "Any government," he said, "is free to the people under it . . . where the laws rule and the people are a party to those laws; and more than that is tyranny, oligarchy, and confusion."

William Penn wrote Pennsylvania's first constitution, calling it a "frame of government." The people of the colony were to elect their general assemblies under this constitutional framework. The Assembly had wide-ranging rights. Under the

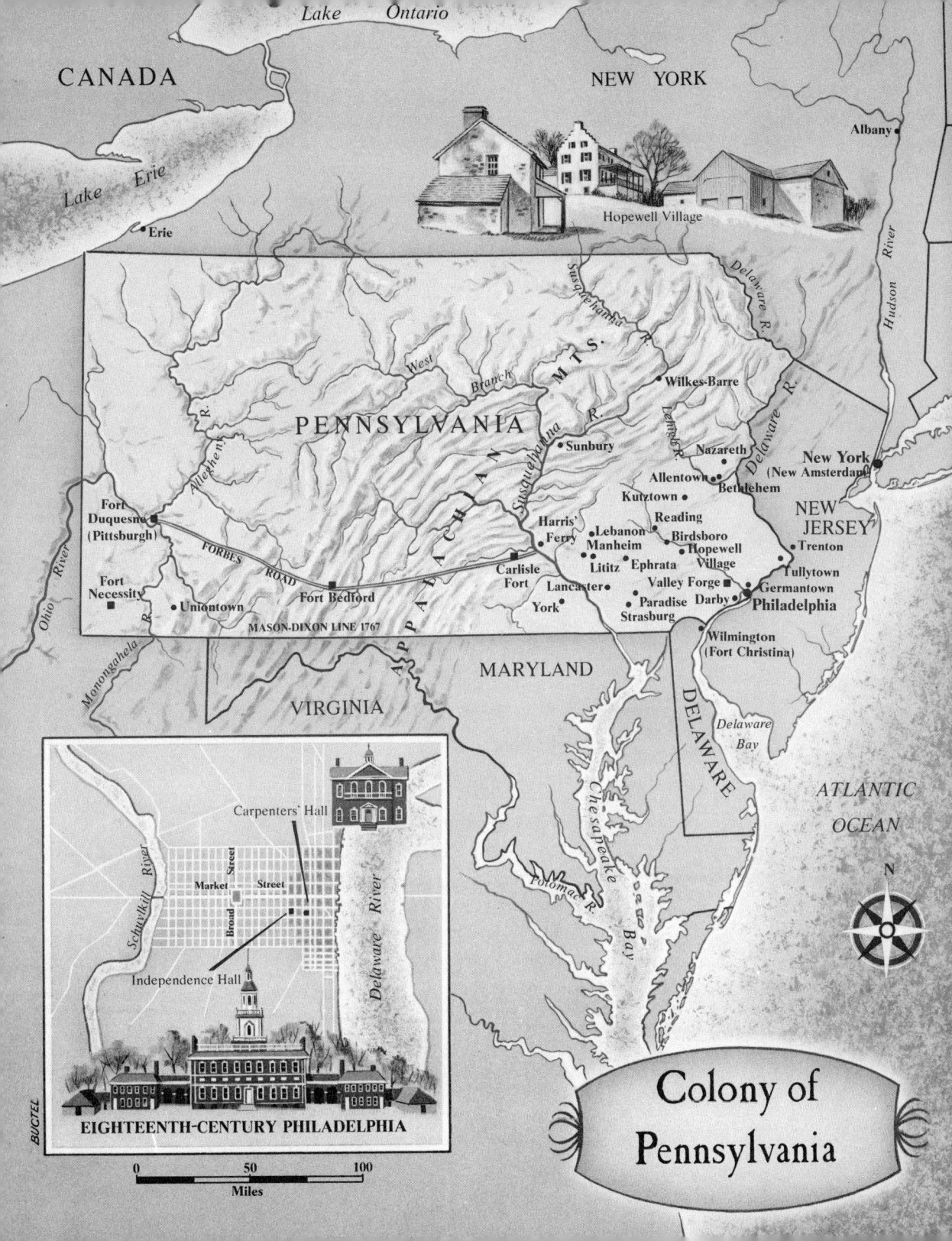

A singing lesson in an early New World school

royal grant, the laws had to be approved by the crown, as in the other proprietary colonies. The former residents—Dutch, Swedes, and Finns—became full-fledged citizens. Total religious freedom was guaranteed: unique, indeed, in that age even in most parts of British North America. The holy experiment was to result in the creation of a "consecrated community" where people would lead lives of integrity, respecting their fellow citizens and taking active parts in a great human adventure.

The declaration of these noble sentiments was just the beginning. Only an educated citizenry could lead the lives the Quakers advocated. Penn included in the constitution a provision for establishing public schools and also indicated that parents and guardians were responsible for their children's being taught to read and write. In fact, it was not until 1834 that the public school system became a reality, as a result of the Free School Act. The Quakers, however, established the first organized school in the colony in 1689. Located in Philadelphia, it was known as the Friends' Public School, and now operates as the William Penn Charter School. Other religious groups set up schools for their children soon after.

Penn's frame of government provided for a deputy governor, whom he (Penn) would appoint, and a council of seventy-two members. In the all-important area of law, it is notable to observe how Penn's humanitarian feelings prevailed. Whereas in Great Britain death was the penalty for some three hundred misdeeds (some of them quite trivial), in Pennsylvania capital punishment could be incurred only for murder and treason.

Before Penn had sailed for his new colony in 1682, he had spent considerable time advertising for settlers. His offer was quite attractive. For $500 the new settler could have an estate of 5,000 acres and a plot of land in Philadelphia, which was to

Bethlehem, Pennsylvania, settled by religious peoples from Europe

be the colony's capital city. For a cent an acre, the settler could rent a 200-acre farm.

Penn's advertising worked, and settlers began to come to the new colony—English, Scotch-Irish, Welsh, Swiss, Dutch, German, and others. Germans eventually made up about one-third of the colony's population. They spoke German, "Deutsch" in their tongue. To the non-German, the word sounded like "Dutch," and so these settlers became known as the "Pennsylvania Dutch." In reality they were (and are) Pennsylvanians of German descent.

Many Pennsylvania Dutch immigrants settled near the Delaware River and then pushed westward to the virgin lands, building communities in the mountainous areas and valleys. Their settlements recalled their European homes or Biblical names—Manheim, Strasburg, Lititz, Kutztown, Bethlehem, Nazareth, Lebanon, Paradise, and others. They were members of many religious sects—Amish, Mennonites, Dunkards (because of their baptismal practices), River Brethren, Brinsers, United Zion Children, and many others. For a long time (and some even today), they kept their old ways in habit and clothing. Theater and dancing were forbidden, as were painted portraits (and later photographs) because they were considered violations of the Biblical warning against "graven images." They continued to speak seventeenth-century German (as many still do). Penn was impressed by their hard work and honesty, and their abilities as clockmakers, glass makers, carpenters, saddlers, textile workers, and blacksmiths, all skills that a new colony desperately needed.

Prominent among the German settlers were those from the town of Crefeld (Krefeld) in the northern Rhine region of Germany. They were skilled in silk-spinning and dyeing. Their main leader was Francis Daniel Pastorius. On a tract of some

15,000 acres, in 1683 he laid out a settlement called Germantown, today a part of the city of Philadelphia known for its quaint and picturesque streets and buildings. Pastorius was also a poet, in his native German as well as in English and Latin. He wrote an English grammar for the German settlers and gave a detailed description of the colony. Elected to the assembly, he was the first mayor of Germantown and an early protestor against the practice of slavery. Pastorius died in Germantown in 1720.

Although Pennsylvania seemed a land of great promise, getting there took great courage. Sailing from Germany, for instance, the voyage could last as long as four months, the ship sometimes tossed about by awesome waves, at other times becalmed with its sails hanging limp in the absence of wind. Besides being boring, life on the ship often became unbearable. Meager portions of salted meat became covered with worms, and water was undrinkable. The passengers suffered from body lice so thick that they had to be scraped off the skin.

In such conditions, it is no wonder that the voyagers came down with all sorts of diseases, among them typhus, scurvy, and dysentery. According to contemporary accounts, children under seven seldom survived the voyage, and many adults also died on the trip.

One sailing vessel left Rotterdam in the Netherlands with four hundred Germans aboard in those early days, headed for the New World. On the way across the Atlantic, the sailing masts broke and the ship's captain died of a heart attack. Three-quarters of the passengers were dead from disease and accidents when the ship reached Long Island Sound. There it ran aground on Block Island, and had to be towed into port. Getting to Pennsylvania, or any of the other colonies, was not a task for the fainthearted.

*Some of the first Quaker settlers
made their homes in the sides of hills.*

But they did come, because the colonies promised a new and better life. Some of the first Quaker settlers made their new homes in caves near the river banks until they could build suitable shelters. "Better a dugout than a dungeon," they said, "better a cave than a loathsome jail."

In spite of all the hardships of travel and early settlement, the immigrants continued to come. Back in Europe, many people could not support themselves and their families. Even in the most advanced nations of Western Europe, death by starvation was common. Many were harassed for their religious beliefs. In Pennsylvania there was religious freedom and much fertile farmland that produced grains, hemp, flax, and a variety of fruits. Besides the venison and fish in abundance, livestock was raised in large numbers. Simple industries began to develop: tanning, saw and grist mills, then papermaking, iron manufacturing, and shipbuilding.

THE CITY OF BROTHERLY LOVE

William Penn first saw his colony in 1682, remaining in Pennsylvania until 1684. Before his arrival he had sent his cousin, Captain William Markham, to the colony. Markham became Pennsylvania's first deputy governor. He carried with him to the New World Penn's plans for the great city of his colony. He named it Philadelphia (the name means "brotherly love" in Greek), and it was to cover 10,000 acres on a plain between the Delaware and Schuylkill rivers. His surveyor, Thomas Holme, actually laid out less than a third of that area. Today Philadelphia covers about 130 square miles.

The city was laid out according to Penn's plans. The streets were broad, at right angles in gridiron fashion. Penn wanted Philadelphia to become a model for future cities in the colonies. (Indeed, by the time of Penn's death in 1718 it was said to be the most beautiful city in North America.) As such, he envisioned each house with a garden and small orchard, but as the city grew the brick houses sprang up wall to wall, lining the streets. Many of these original homes have been preserved in the older section of the modern city.

Holme named Philadelphia's streets for famous people, but Penn objected to this. Instead, he numbered the streets running north and south, and gave the names of trees and flowers to the intersecting streets—Chestnut, Walnut, Spruce, Pine, Sassafras, Vine. They are still among Philadelphia's most famous street names.

By August of 1683 about eighty families were housed in Philadelphia. Two years later the population had grown to 2,500. When Penn returned to the colony in 1699, his city had about 4,500 people. (With a population of around two million, Philadelphia ranks as the fourth largest city in the United States today.) Elfreth Alley in Philadelphia is said to be the nation's oldest residential street.

According to Gabriel Thomas in his *An Historical and Geographical Account of the Province and Country of Pennsylvania, 1698*, the City of Brotherly Love had a "noble Town House or Guild Hall, a handsome market house, and a convenient prison," as well as two warehouses, malt- and brew-houses, bakehouses, and "no beggars or old maids."

Even Penn could not have dreamed how important a role his city of Philadelphia would play in the history of America. From 1683 until 1799 Philadelphia was the capital of the colony. From 1775 to 1789, and again from 1790 to 1800, it was the capital of the country.

From their original cave dwellings, the Quakers and other hard-working settlers moved into clapboard houses, and then many of them into stone mansions. The more wealthy people had homes on Front Street, facing the river. Some of the houses had balconies, and several were furnished with pieces ordered directly from England.

The Quakers and other Pennsylvania colonists turned out to be good traders. But their attitude toward money was somewhat different from that of the New England colonists to the north. The Puritans held that wealth was God's reward for an individual's hard work. The wealthier a man, therefore, the more virtuous he was supposed to be. The Quakers held no such beliefs. They did not relate wealth to virtue. But just the same, many of them made money. Increasingly, Philadelphia and Pennsylvania entered the world of trade—with Great Britain and other British colonies and later with other countries. Lumber, tobacco, grain, horses, wool, and meat began to leave the colony in increasing numbers. By 1685 Philadelphia had its own printing press and was soon printing its own newspaper, the *American Weekly Mercury*.

Besides William Penn, and later Benjamin Franklin, the city of Philadelphia could list many prominent names. Among them was John Bartram (1699–1779), a botanist born near Darby, Pennsylvania. In 1731 he started a garden near Philadelphia and made experiments in hybridizing (crossing different plants to create improved species). His garden, now a part of the city's park system, still contains many huge trees which Bartram himself planted. His son William (1739–1823) carried on his work.

The engraving on pages 42–43 shows (top) Philadelphia as seen from the New Jersey colony; (bottom left) a plan for the city's streets; and (bottom right) the Battery and State House.

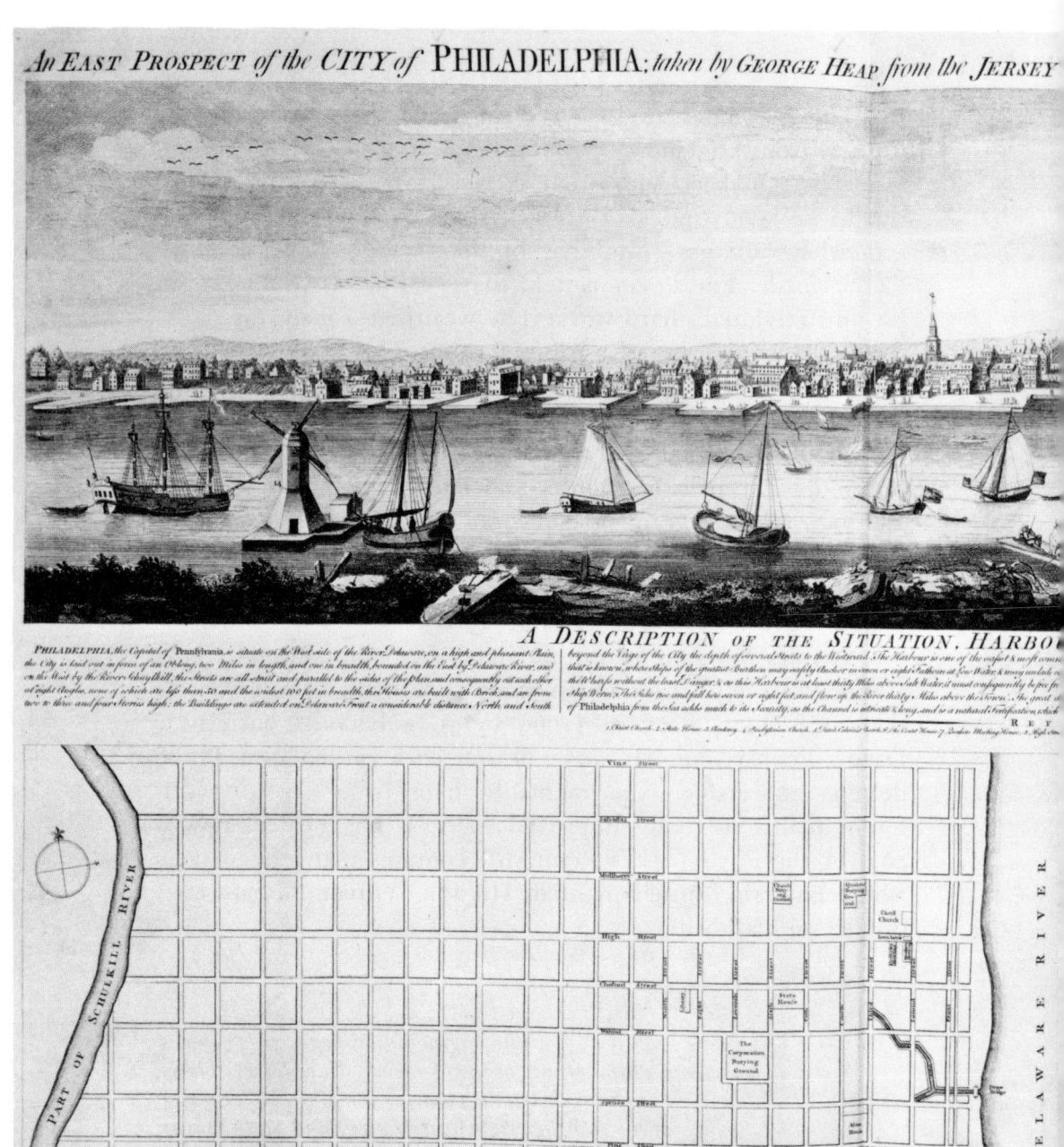

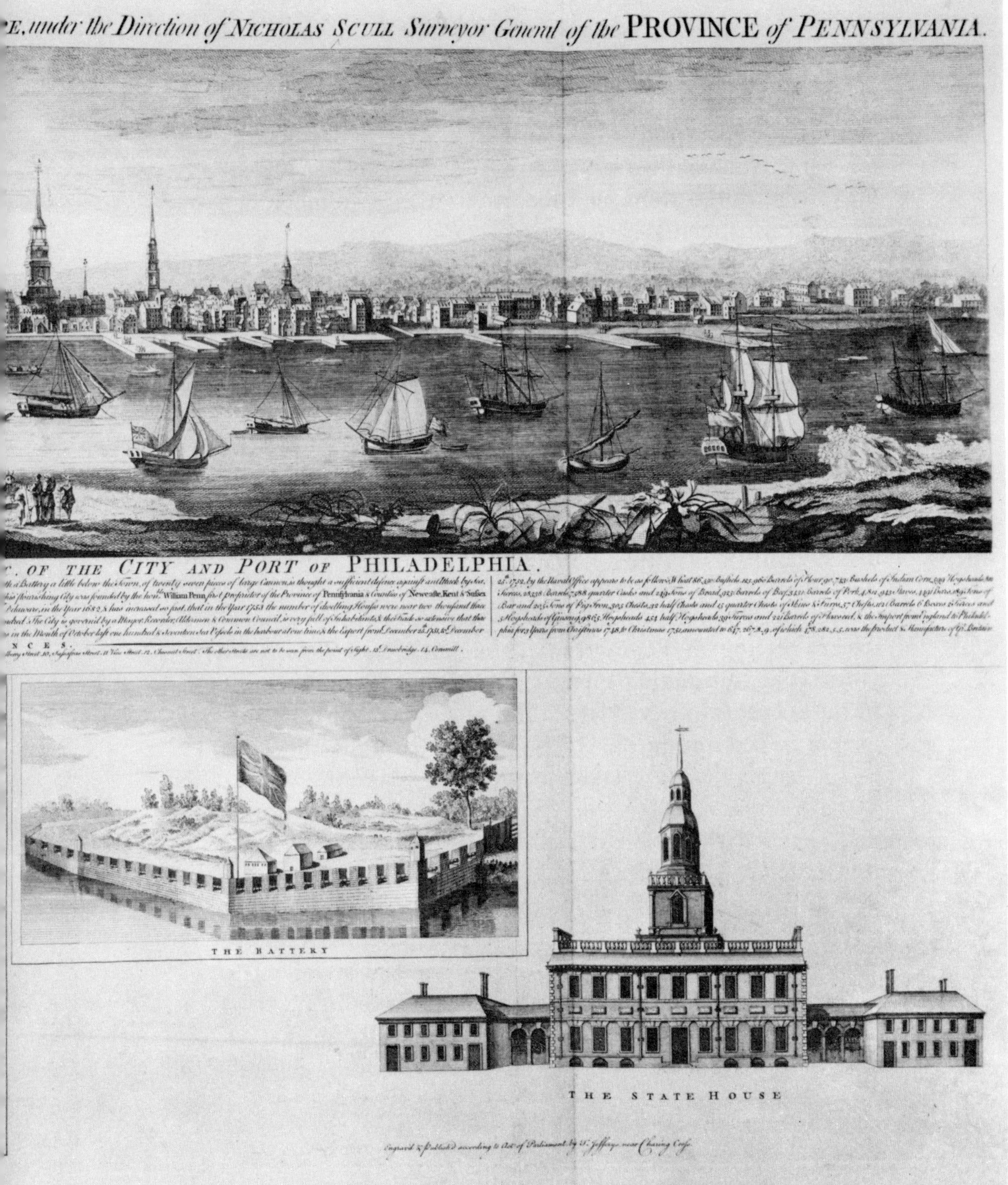

e, under the Direction of NICHOLAS SCULL Surveyor General of the PROVINCE of PENNSYLVANIA.

... OF THE CITY AND PORT OF PHILADELPHIA.

THE BATTERY

THE STATE HOUSE

Philip Syng Physick (1768–1837), known as the "Father of American Surgery," was born in Philadelphia, too. He became famous for operations to remove stones from the bladder and for using animal ligatures (cords used as threads) in surgery. He invented the stomach tube, as well as a number of other surgical instruments.

Dr. Benjamin Rush was born near Philadelphia around 1745. The author of several medical books, he was among the first to recognize the dangers of tooth infection and contributed to the establishment of Philadelphia as a center of medical training.

Although William Penn envisioned equality for all in his city and colony, of course that was not fully realized. Some people grew rich by legal and other means; some stayed poor; and some grew destitute. At the bottom of the social scale were the indentured servants and slaves. Indentured servants contracted to work for a certain number of years in return for passage to the colony. Although there was always much antislavery feeling in Pennsylvania, the settlers of Penn's colony, Quakers included, did own some slaves. But the number of slaves in the colony was never large, and in Germantown in 1688 the people passed an antislavery resolution. In 1780 the Assembly passed a law stating that no child born in Pennsylvania after that time would be a slave. Except for Vermont's constitution three years earlier, that was the first antislavery law passed in any state.

While the City of Brotherly Love continued to grow and prosper, so did the rest of Penn's colony. Pennsylvania Dutch farmers especially spread out over the land. The tall, spacious, sprawling barns they built are still typical of the Pennsylvania farm country. These barns originated in the Rhine Valley, and were used for storing farm products, such as grain and tobacco.

The interiors of the farmhouses also looked very much like homes back in Germany. Even today in Pennsylvania it is possible to see German-language tablets on the walls of farmhouses reading *Friede auf Erden* (Peace on Earth)—William Penn's most fervent hope.

Penn wrote a prayer for his city in 1684. Today it can be read on a plaque in City Hall Plaza, and perhaps it best expresses his feeling toward his creation. It reads: "And thou Philadelphia, the virgin settlement of this province named before thou wert born, what love, what care, what service and what travail has there been to bring thee forth and preserve thee from such as would abuse and defile thee. O that thou mayest be kept from the evil that would overwhelm thee, that, faithful to the God of thy mercies, in the life of righteousness, thou mayest be preserved to the end. My soul prays to God for thee that thou mayest stand in the day of trial, that thy children may be blest of the Lord, and thy people saved by His power."

Even after Penn's death, the Pennsylvania colonists continued in various ways to express great pride in their major city. In 1751 a bell was ordered from the Whitechapel Foundry in London to be hung in the tower of the new State House (now Independence Hall). It arrived in September of 1752, weighing over 2,000 pounds, three feet from lip to crown, and twelve feet around the lip. Inscribed on the bell are the words "Proclaim Liberty Throughout All the Land unto All the Inhabitants Thereof. Lev. XXV, 10." Below that was inscribed "By order of the Assembly of the Province of Pennsylvania for the State House in the City of Philadelphia." The inscription also contains the names of the founders and the date.

While the new bell was being tested, it cracked. It was recast by two local workmen, Pass and Stow, whose names also appear on the bell. In the recasting, American copper was

A view of Penn's city of brotherly love in 1777

added to the original metal so that it would not be so brittle. That did not seem to work at first because the second bell was defective, and so a third was cast. It was hung in the tower in 1753 and rung for the first time to convene the Assembly in August of that year.

The Liberty Bell did not receive its present name until 1839. Some other important dates in the life of the bell were July 8, 1776, when it was rung to announce the adoption of the Declaration of Independence (July 4); September, 1777, when it was taken down and hidden from the British in Allentown, Pennsylvania, during the American Revolution; 1778, when it was returned to the State House tower; and 1783, when it became known as the Independence Bell.

On July 8, 1835, the Independence Bell was rung for the funeral of Chief Justice John Marshall, and it cracked. Repaired, it kept ringing until Washington's birthday, 1846, when it cracked once again. That time it could not be fixed. The Liberty Bell now hangs in a frame above a platform inside Independence Hall. In preparation for the bicentennial celebration of American independence (1976), plans were made to move the bell to a spot on Independence Mall. It was thought that the Liberty Bell's chances of survival against the expected crush of visitors were greater on the mall.

THE QUAKERS AND THE INDIANS

As we know, Columbus gave the name "Indians" to the native people living in North America in the mistaken belief that he had found the subcontinent of India. Other mistaken ideas about these native Americans have persisted until present times. It was assumed that the Indians had occupied the American continent since the beginnings of their civilization. It was also believed that the Indians were members of a fourth race, besides the white, black, and yellow; and so they were called red men. As it turned out, neither assumption is true.

The American Indian's ancestors were not members of a "red" race. They were of Asian Mongolian origin, and, therefore, part of the so-called yellow race. And many centuries ago they came from Asia—Siberia and Mongolia—to the North American continent. Hunters, they followed the animal herds who roamed the cold lands of northern Asia. At some point in the past (perhaps as much as 35,000 years ago), they may have crossed the Bering Strait, the narrow body of water which separates Asia from Alaska and the North American continent. The two land areas might have been joined at that time.

Once they reached the American continent, and still following the herds, the Mongolian tribes began to move southward. Anthropologists have found evidence of their civilization left behind in graves. A nomadic people, they moved frequently to wherever the hunting and fishing were best.

Finally, the Mongolian tribes reached Central and South America, too, where they established the great empires of the Incas, Mayas, and others, reaching a high degree of civilization. When the white men reached the American continent and began to explore it, these empires were quickly crushed.

It is not known how many "Indians" lived on the American continent when the white man first arrived. Some guesses say about one million. It is estimated that perhaps 15,000 Indians lived in Pennsylvania when it became a colony. Like the other tribes scattered over the continent, the Indians in Pennsylvania had, through the centuries, gone through many changes in their ways of life. In the far-distant past, they had hunted the huge mammoths that roamed the land, using stone spears to kill the beasts. After the mammoths became extinct, the Indians turned food-gathers and fishermen, as well as hunters. About 3,000 years ago, the Indians also became farmers. They grew corn, beans, and squash among other vegetables, and also learned to make pottery.

Penn and other Quakers thought that the Indians in America might be part of the "lost ten tribes" of the ancient Hebrews. They noted some likenesses between the ways of both groups. Both Indian and Jew observed the lunar calendar, adjusted to the earth's movements around the sun. Pennsylvania

Indians also observed a harvest festival that reminded the Quakers of the Jews' Feast of the Tabernacle in the fall.

True to his Quaker beliefs, Penn regarded the Indians as fellow human beings. His first letter to an Indian chief in southeast Pennsylvania was written from Europe.

"The Great God," he wrote, "who is the power that made you and me, inclines your heart to righteousness, love and peace with one another, which I hope the Great God will incline both you and me to do . . . I have already taken care that none of my people shall sell rum to make your people drunk . . . I am your loving friend, William Penn. England, the 21st of the second month, 1682."

Penn also gave instructions that the Indians in Pennsylvania should not be cheated. He wanted to make sure that they understood what they were being offered in exchange for their land. Unfortunately, Penn's wishes were not always observed.

During the second year of Penn's first visit to his colony, he made a peace treaty with the Indians of Pennsylvania. Following their religious beliefs, Quakers will take no oaths, but consider their oral pledge as binding. Later, the great French author Voltaire, a man not in the habit of handing out compliments, said of this agreement between Penn and the native Americans, "This was the only pact never sworn to and never broken."

At the time of the settlement of Pennsylvania, there were probably about forty-five Indian tribes in the colony. The majority were part of the Algonquian family. Their name means "at the place of spearing fish," which indicates how they got much of their food supply and how important it was to them.

William Penn's warm and friendly letter to an Indian chief in southeastern Pennsylvania

The Great God who is the power and wisdom that made you and me Incline your hearts to Righteousness Love and peace. This I send to Assure you of my Love, and to desire your Love to my friends, and when the Great God brings me among you I Intend to order all things in such manner that we may all live in Love and peace one with another which I hope the Great God will Incline both me and you to do. I seek nothing but the honor of his name, and that we who are his workmanship, may do that which is well pleasing to him. The man which delivers this unto you, is my special friend, sober wise and Loving, you may believe him. I have already taken care that none of my people wrong you, by good Laws I have provided for that purpose, nor will I ever allow any of my people to sell Rumme to make your people drunk. If anything should be out of order, expect when I come, it shall be mended, and I will bring you some things of our Country that are useful and pleasing to you. So I rest In y Love of our god y made us I am

England 21 : 2 mo : 1682

Your Loveing freind

WM PENN

I sent this to the Indians by an Interpr. ye 6 mo 1682
Tho: Holme

This engraving depicts an Indian massacre at Lancaster, Pennsylvania, in 1763.

Another important tribe was the Lenni Lenape, also known as the Delaware. Their name means "original people." Perhaps for this reason, and also because they were a peace-loving people who tried to settle differences between tribes, they were also called the "Grandfathers" by other Indians.

The Pennsylvania Indians were a short, light-skinned people. They did not have domesticated animals, and lived simply, their homes being lean-tos made of trees and tree bark. They grew and smoked tobacco, which might be the reason why many of them died young from throat and lung ailments.

At first, most of the tribes in the Pennsylvania colony were friendly and generous to the white settlers. They grew to trust and respect William Penn. But Penn was not always in his colony, and not all of those (including Quakers) who lived in Pennsylvania felt as he did. Despite laws to the contrary, the colonists sold liquor to the Indians, who were unused to drinking. They killed many of the so-called "savages" in petty disputes, placating their consciences by saying that Indians were not Christians and, therefore, not under the protection of the laws of God. They cheated the Indians in land sales, too. The Indians in Pennsylvania had a unique way of determining how much land a certain measure contained—it was the amount a man could walk around in a single day. When the settlers learned of this, they hired sturdy young men, paced by horses, to run around the land. Too late, the Indians realized that they were being fooled.

Such practices were not unique to Pennsylvania, but occurred throughout all the colonies. At length even such peace-loving people as the Lenni Lenape exploded in violence on occasion, protesting their treatment by the white men. Even George III of Great Britain, who came to the throne in 1760 and was not known for his humanitarian sentiments, felt compelled at one point to issue a royal proclamation for the protection of the Indians. He said in it that the several nations and tribes "who live under our protection should not be molested or disturbed in the possession of the royal domains reserved for them."

Finally, Indian and white man in the British colonies became involved in all-out wars. One of these, known as the French and Indian War, 1754–63, pitted Great Britain and its colonies in the New World against France, its Canadian colonies, and its American Indian allies. For self-protection, the gentle Lenni Lenape joined the warlike Iroquois, who assigned them the role usually given to Indian women—they were not allowed to fight or take part in tribal councils.

The war began when French Canadians built Fort Duquesne (on the site of what is now Pittsburgh, Pennsylvania). A twenty-two-year-old army officer by the name of George Washington was sent by the colony of Virginia to evict the Canadians because Virginia claimed that territory.

Washington and his men were attacked and defeated by a force of Canadians and Indians. During the years of this war, which was a prelude to the Seven Years' War, 1756–63, between France and Britain and their allies in Europe, battles were fought up and down the northern colonies in the New World. Canadians and Indians made many raids into the colony of Pennsylvania. Finally, the British were victorious in both land and sea battles.

The Treaty of Paris (February 8, 1763) ended both the war in the colonies and that in Europe, leaving Great Britain as the world's leading colonial power. But it brought changes to the colonists and the Indians as well. The American colonists gained much confidence in themselves by fighting alongside British regulars. But the native Americans did not fare so well. With the victory, Britain's colonial policy toward the Indians hastened the death of the free Indian nations in North America. Unlike the French, who sought to live side by side with the different culture of the Indians, the British—as the Americans did later—tried to, and in some ways did, absorb them into the white culture, thereby destroying the Indians' own culture and way of life.

TROUBLE IN ENGLAND AND THE COLONY

Although there was much to do in his new colony, William Penn was forced to return to England in 1684 to take care of business and other matters. In 1685 James II, the former Duke of York, took the throne upon the death of his brother, Charles II. Since Penn was a good friend of the new king, he was in a position to secure the release of many persecuted Quakers and to gain other favors. But the friendship also hurt Penn. James was a devout Roman Catholic in a Protestant land. That led to his forced departure (December, 1688) from the throne in England's "Glorious Revolution," which settled once and for all the question of the country's official religion. The Church of England was the established church.

Protestants William and Mary came to the throne in February, 1689—he the king of the Netherlands and grandson of Charles I, she the daughter of James II. Under their rule, Penn was accused of being in sympathy with the Catholics and of engaging in "treasonable correspondence" with the banished former king. He was acquitted of the charge.

During this period, 1692–94, while Penn was charged with these offenses, his colony in America was taken from him and annexed to New York. After his acquittal, it was restored to him.

The year of his acquittal, Penn's wife died. In 1696 he entered into another marriage. His second wife was Hannah Callowhill, of a Bristol family. They had eight children, but three died in infancy.

During these years Penn did much writing and continued to work in the interests of his Quaker beliefs and in the cause of peace. In 1697 he presented to the London Board of Trade a plan for the union of the American colonies. He wrote *An Essay Towards the Present and Future Peace of Europe* (1693), in which he proposed the prevention of war by establishing an organization of countries (a sort of United Nations long before the present one). He also wrote pamphlets and books on philosophical and religious topics.

In 1699, with his wife and secretary, James Logan, Penn returned again to Pennsylvania. Much had changed in his absence. Philadelphia had become the largest and richest city in the colonies, as many of the old settlers had acquired great wealth. Some of the new settlers looked upon the Indians as savages and slaves. Also, the Pennsylvania Assembly was in constant disagreement with the lieutenant governors and with their Councils, whom they accused of high-handed actions. Some of the Quakers refused to provide military defenses, which made the home government in England unhappy.

With his talent for dealing with people and depending on his own sense of fairness, Penn was able to settle many of his young colony's problems—at least temporarily. However, he was forced to allow the "lower counties," in which the Quakers were in a minority, to set up their own type of government, linked with the others only through the governor. Penn also agreed to a new constitution in 1701, known as the Charter of Privileges. It extended the political rights of the people.

Penn was obliged once more to return to England in 1701. (He left Logan to manage his colonial affairs, which the secretary did for about half a century.) Penn had heard of trouble once more at court. William was still on the throne, Mary having died in 1694. The king needed money to strengthen his military forces, and one of the ways he hoped to get it was by converting the British proprietary colonies into crown colonies. This would mean that the government in London, not Penn, would rule over Pennsylvania. (William died in 1702, and Pennsylvania remained a proprietary colony until the Revolution.)

Penn was never again to see his beloved "holy experiment," and his last years in England were far from happy. He continued to hear of conflicts between the lieutenant governors and the citizens in his colony. Many of his officials were incompetent. The Assembly, too, continued to quarrel with the Council. One of Penn's stewards (business agents) swindled him so completely that he (Penn) was forced to spend nine months in debtor's prison in 1707–08.

All these misfortunes proved too much even for so capable and strong a man. In 1712 William Penn suffered a paralyzing stroke. He died five years later on July 30, 1718, at the age of seventy-four, and is buried in the Quaker burying ground in Buckinghamshire, England.

After his stroke, Penn's wife managed his private and colonial affairs for a time. From 1732–41, their son Thomas ran the colony. A grandson, John, was lieutenant governor of Penn-

*Penn's second and last visit
to his colony, 1699*

BY THE HONOURABLE COLLONEL
John Evans LIEUTENANT GOVERNOUR of the PROVINCE OF PENSILVANIA AND COUNTIES ANNEXED.

A PROCLAMATION,
AGAINST IMMORALITY and PROPHANENESS

Whereas it hath pleased ALMIGHTY GOD, from the Treasures of His Infinite Goodness to extend its favours in an eminent degree, and pour down His peculiar Blessings upon this Colony, from the first Erecting thereof; as well by the bestowing a happy success on the Endeavours of its Inhabitants, and crowning what so lately was a Wilderness with a large Affluence of all the Necessaries and Comforts of Life; as by supporting it in an undisturbed Peace and Tranquility during the Commotions that have deeply afflicted other parts of the Christian World, and continuing to us the Enjoyment of those manifold Mercies which, rightly used, tend to make a People truly happy. All which divine Bounties, as they loudly call for the most humble and hearty acknowledgments, so they ought more deeply to impress a just sense of the great Obligations upon Us, so to regulate our Lives with care and circumspection, in a true Obedience and Conformity to God's holy Laws, that we may not instead of making grateful Returns by Impiety or Negligence, provoke the just Anger of the ALMIGHTY to withdraw His divine Protection, and inflict on us the severe Chastisements of his just Displeasure. Notwithstanding all which, I cannot but be sensible, that too many, forgetting all those Obligations, that as persons professing the Holy Christian Religion they indispensably lye under, have given themselves a Loose in their Lives and Conversations, and manifestly trampled on their positive known Duties in many vicious Practices and Immoralities to the great Offence of ALMIGHTY GOD, in the Breach of his Divine Laws as well as of our civil Institutions and to the scandal of sober Men, and great Discredit of this Government: Which Practices if not timely prevented, may terminate in an utter Depravation of Manners, through the Encouragement taken from those fatal and pernicious Examples, by persons whose better Education and Inclinations might otherwise have restrained them within the Bounds of Sobriety and Virtue; but from those many Instances, sett before their Eyes, are in danger of being hurried on, not only to their own Ruine, but of becoming Accessary to the Incensing, and drawing down upon us the Vengeance of Heaven.

In a deep Consideration of which, and to the end that all possible Discouragements may be given to the Growth of these Enormities; I have through a sense of the Duty I owe to GOD, and the care of the People committed to my Charge, and with the Advice and Consent of the Council of this Province and Territories Though fit to Publish and Declare That I will Discountenance and severely Punish all manner of Vice, Immorality and Prophaneness, in all persons whatsoever, within this Government, that shall be guilty of the same. And I doe hereby strictly forbid all manner of Debauchery, Lewdness, Drunkenness, prophane Swearing, Cursing, Rioting, or breaking of the Sabboth, Night-walking at unseasonable hours without lawfull Business, & all other Disorders Whatsoever that are contrary to the Duties of a Christian Life & the Rules of true Virtue. And I do strictly Command & Require all Magistrates, Justices, Sheriffs, Constables and all Officers whatsoever, and other her Majesties good Subjects that they not only be regular and circumspect in their own Lives that by their good Examples, they may incite those that behold them to the Practice of virtue, but also that they be very Diligent in the Discovery and Effectual Prosecution of all Offenders, and that they rigorously put in Execution all the good and wholesome Laws and Ordinances provided against the aforesaid and such other Immoralities without favour, shew, or affection to any person whatsoever as they will answer it to Almighty God and incur my utmost Displeasure.

And for the more effectual Prosecution hereof I do require and Command the Justices of Quarter Sessions in their respective Counties in this Government and the Mayor and Recorder of the City of Philadelphia, that they cause this my Proclamation to be publickly read in open Court, immediately after their Charge is given to the grand-Jury.

And that the Ministers of all Churches and several Congregations within this Province and Territories, cause the same to be Read in the time of Divine Service, at their respective places of Worship at least six times in every Year. And that they be very Diligent in Discouraging all manner of Vice, and Immorality in their Auditors and Exhorting them to the Exercise of piety and virtue.

Given at Philadelphia the Ninth day of October man... at a... the Reign of our Sovereign Lady ANN by the Grace of GOD of England, Scotland, France and Ireland Queen Defender of the Faith &c. And the twenty fourth of the Proprietaries Government Annoq: Domini 1704.

JOHN EVANS.

God Save the Queen.

sylvania from 1763–71 and 1773–76; and another grandson, Richard, served as lieutenant governor from 1771–73.

Pennsylvania did not turn out to be the total ideal that Penn had envisioned, nor perhaps was it even a successful "holy experiment." But many colonials agreed with the view that William Penn was the greatest leader ever to govern an American colony. Certainly he was a man of intellect and integrity, who tried his best all his life.

A proclamation issued by one of Penn's lieutenant governors, 1704

FRANKLIN AND THE REVOLUTION

If the colony of Pennsylvania's first citizen was William Penn, certainly another citizen, Benjamin Franklin (1706–90), was no less distinguished. Diplomat, author, scientist, printer, philosopher, and inventor, Franklin was remarkably successful in each field.

Born in Boston, Franklin reached Philadelphia in 1723, where he went to work as a printer at the age of seventeen. Nine years later he began to attain fame as the publisher of *Poor Richard's Almanack* (1732–57). Under the pen name of Richard Saunders, he showed a kind of homespun American morality with such thoughts as "A great empire, like a great cake, is most easily diminished at the edges."

Franklin's contributions to his adopted city and colony, and later to his country, are almost endless. He formed the discussion group Junto in 1727, which became the American Philosophical Society (1743). In 1731 he laid the foundations for what developed into the Philadelphia Public Library

The Merchants' Exchange, Philadelphia, built in *1702* and shown here in *1754*, was originally a private home and later the resort of the city's wealthy people.

(chartered in 1742). He improved the lighting of the city's streets. He was its deputy postmaster. He was the leader in establishing an academy (1749) that later became the University of Pennsylvania, a city hospital and an insurance company (both in 1751). He invented the lightning rod in his famous kite experiments of 1752. In his spare time he taught himself Spanish, Latin, and French.

At first intensely loyal to the British crown, Franklin entered public life in his forties. Through his career it is possible to follow the steps that led to the American Revolution.

In 1751 Franklin was elected to the Pennsylvania Assembly, becoming a leader in the dominant Quaker party. During the French and Indian War, he led a military expedition to the Lehigh Valley and influenced the Assembly to allocate money for defense and to appoint commissioners to conduct a full-scale war. In 1757 Pennsylvania sent him to London as the colony's agent. After five years he was back again in America, organizing its postal system and serving for a time as deputy postmaster general. Over the next fifteen years he fought for Pennsylvania's, and all the other colonies', rights and interests, gradually changing from staunch Englishman to dedicated American.

By the 1760s, with George III on the throne, the relationship between Great Britain and its American colonies had changed considerably. Since the first settlements, the colonies had been thought of as the king's possessions. Parliament actually had little control over them except to regulate trade. Through the growing years, the settlers began more and more to think of themselves as Americans and to want a larger measure of self-government. They did not at first have any notion of becoming a separate country. Instead, they called for their "rights" as Englishmen, most importantly the power to tax themselves. But a series of taxes by the British Parliament brought the colonies and the mother country closer and closer to a showdown and then to war.

In 1765 Parliament passed the Stamp Act, requiring the colonists to buy stamps for newspapers, licenses, and other legal documents. The colonists thought this an unfair use of royal power. Franklin was in England at the time. Although against the Stamp Act, he did feel that it must be obeyed. The colonists at home, however, felt differently. A so-called Stamp Act Congress met in New York in October, 1765, and John Dickinson, then of Pennsylvania, led the fight for repeal of the act. The British Parliament yielded and repealed the Stamp Act in March of the following year, which encouraged Franklin to hope for improved relations between England and the colonies. Soon he was discouraged once again.

It was obvious in 1767 that Parliament had no intention of heeding the colonists' cry for "no taxation without representation," when it passed the Townshend Acts. These called for taxes on paper, tea, and other items. It was at this point that Franklin truly became American rather than English. He denounced the Townshend Acts, declaring, at least in private, that they might cause the colonies to revolt. People listened to what Franklin said. He was certainly the leading spokesman for the colonies in England. By 1770 he had also become the agent for the colonies of Georgia, New Jersey, and Massachusetts.

Except for the tax on tea, Parliament repealed the Townshend Acts in March, 1770. But now even this did not satisfy the restive colonists. They demanded that the tax on tea be removed also. When it was not, they began to take matters into their own hands. In 1773 a ship delivering tea to Philadelphia was stopped downriver and ordered to return. In December of that year some Boston citizens disguised as Indians dumped

overboard the cargo of tea from three ships in the harbor. George III reacted by passing the Intolerable Acts of 1774. Among other things, these acts closed the port of Boston.

The colonists decided on a new plan. Delegates from all the colonies except Georgia met in Philadelphia in September, 1774, in the First Continental Congress. They voiced their grievances but did not call for independence. After demanding repeal of all objectionable acts passed by Parliament, the Congress decided to meet again in 1775 if Great Britain did not yield.

In March of 1775 Franklin was on his way home. Insulted in England and called a traitor, he could no longer work effectively, especially after such incidents as the Boston Tea Party.

Benjamin Franklin had come home at a crucial time. In April, 1775, George III sent British troops to destroy supplies of arms that the colonists had gathered in Massachusetts. At Lexington on April 19, British soldiers and American colonists voiced their differences once again, this time with muskets. The American Revolution had begun.

Franklin served in the Second Continental Congress, convened in May, 1775, in the State House at Philadelphia. The delegates issued one last plea to George III to hear their arguments. The king refused and declared the colonies to be in open rebellion. In December of that year the Parliament in London ordered a naval blockade of America. The following January, Thomas Paine (then living in Philadelphia) issued his pamphlet *Common Sense,* which called for outright independence, stirringly declaring separation to be right and just.

Pennsylvania's distinguished citizen, Benjamin Franklin

On July 4, 1776, the Congress approved the Declaration of Independence, which Franklin helped to draft and also signed. (Nine delegates in all signed for Pennsylvania.) The colonies were now declared to be the United States of America.

The following October, Franklin, along with Silas Deane and Arthur Lee, journeyed to France to seek help for the new nation. Taking his two grandchildren with him, he embarked on a new career as one of the most successful diplomats in history. He was greatly responsible for French aid in money and materials. In fact, he was so successful in obtaining loans from the French that their treasury nearly went bankrupt in the process. One of America's fighting ships, outfitted by the French, was named the *Bonhomme Richard* (Franklin's nickname in French) in Franklin's honor.

When in 1781 the British realized they could not win the war, Franklin talked in secret with English peace negotiators. He also outlined provisions of the eventual peace treaty, including complete independence, a western boundary on the Mississippi River, and removal of all British troops from occupied areas. Along with John Adams and John Jay, Franklin was in great measure responsible for the satisfactory peace treaty the Americans signed in 1783.

Two years after the peace, Franklin was back home once again. Now eighty years old, he was as active as ever as president of Pennsylvania for three years, as well as working for many civic causes and continuing his writings. He even managed to attend the Constitutional Convention in 1787. Franklin

Thomas Paine declared that separation was right and just for the colonies.

lived to see the Constitution ratified, which he urged Pennsylvania to do, and to see his colleague of many years, George Washington, elected as the first president of the United States. No less a statesman and dedicated American was Benjamin Franklin, who died in Philadelphia on April 17, 1790.

The treaty ending the American Revolution.
John Jay stands to the left, Franklin next to him.

THE WAY TO STATEHOOD

The American Revolution began in Massachusetts in 1775 and ended with the signing of a peace treaty in Paris in 1783. With its end, the thirteen English colonies in America became the thirteen states of the United States of America.

Pennsylvania was the scene of fierce battle during the Revolution. The British were especially interested in occupying it because Philadelphia was in a sense the capital city of the rebellious colonies.

The first major battle on Pennsylvania soil took place at Brandywine, about twenty-five miles southwest of Philadelphia, on September 11, 1777. About 15,000 British troops, led by General William Howe, faced George Washington's 11,000 men. (General Washington had become commander-in-chief of the Continental Army in July, 1775.) The Americans lost the battle, leaving open the route for the British to enter Philadelphia, which they did.

On October 4, Washington once again faced Howe, this time at Germantown, now a part of Philadelphia. Once again the Americans were defeated, and the British retained the city.

General Washington and his men suffered greatly during their winter encampment (1777–78) at Valley Forge, twenty miles northwest of Philadelphia. Congress had not made adequate provisions for the army.

During the rest of the war until the decisive British defeat at Yorktown, Virginia, during September and October, 1781, Pennsylvania experienced some fighting, mainly in the Susquehanna River valley. Indians had joined with British loyalists to make trouble for settlers in the area.

The American Revolution, virtually ended at Yorktown, was formally ended with the treaty of 1783. Now began the equally difficult task of forming a united nation.

Wary of a strong central authority, each state, although recognizing that union was necessary, was unwilling to give too much power to a central government. In 1777 the Continental Congress had adopted the Articles of Confederation, which were ratified in 1781. But it was soon evident that the Articles were far too weak to be effective in governing a new nation spread over a large territory. This led to the forming of a Constitutional Convention, which met in Philadelphia from May 25 to September 17, 1787.

Benjamin Franklin was among the Pennsylvania delegates at the convention. In fact, Pennsylvania had more delegates than did any of the other states. There was opposition to the proposed Constitution in Pennsylvania, as there was in the other states. But Franklin and others worked hard to persuade the Pennsylvania delegates to approve it.

On December 12, 1787, Pennsylvania approved the new

Constitution by a vote of forty-six to twenty-three. Delaware had done so five days earlier, so the former colony of Pennsylvania became the second state in the new United States of America.

After having been the capital of Pennsylvania from 1763 to 1799, Philadelphia became the capital of the United States from 1790 to 1800. This main city of William Penn's "holy experiment" lived up to many of his expectations as the early leader in the antislavery movement. And as the site of the American Declaration of Independence and the framing of the Constitution of the United States, Pennsylvania justified its motto of "Virtue, Liberty, and Independence."

An engraving of convention delegate Benjamin Franklin showing him at work on his writings

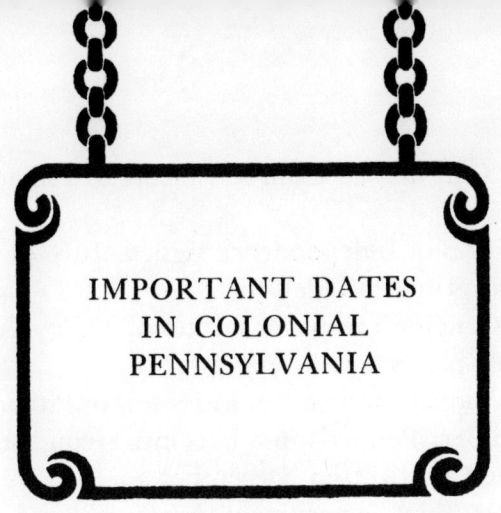

IMPORTANT DATES IN COLONIAL PENNSYLVANIA

1681: Charles II signs charter granting William Penn colony of Pennsylvania, March 4.

1682: Penn drafts Pennsylvania's first constitution, called "frame of government"; draws plans for city of Philadelphia; sees colony for first time.

1683: Philadelphia settled; Penn makes treaty with Indians.

1689: First organized (by Quakers) school in colony.

1699: Penn visits colony for second time.

1701: New constitution, Charter of Privileges, issued.

1754–63: French and Indian War involves Pennsylvania.

1767: Southern boundary settled by famous Mason and Dixon Line.

1769–84: Pennamite Wars.

1774: First Continental Congress meets in Philadelphia, September 5.

1775: Second Continental Congress meets in Philadelphia, May 10.

1776: Declaration of Independence signed, July 4.

1777: British capture Philadelphia.

1777–78: Washington camps for winter at Valley Forge.

1780: Assembly passes antislavery law.

1787: Constitutional Convention in session in Philadelphia, May to September; Pennsylvania becomes second state in union by signing Constitution, December 12.

1790–1800: National government headquartered in Philadelphia.

SOME COLONIAL SIGHTS IN MODERN PENNSYLVANIA

The Commonwealth of Pennsylvania is rich in treasures from the colonial era. Listed below are some of the colonial sights to be seen today in the Keystone State.

Philadelphia
Carpenters' Hall—meeting place of First Continental Congress.
Independence Hall—Declaration of Independence adopted; Constitution framed; Liberty Bell hangs.

Birdsboro
Hopewell village—examples of eighteenth and nineteenth century iron-making villages.

Ephrata
Cornwall iron mine, began operating around 1740.

Erie
Reconstructed home of General Anthony Wayne, leader in American Revolution.

Lancaster County
Home of the Pennsylvania Dutch, where people retain seventeenth-century customs, religion, and dress.

Tullytown
Pennsbury Manor—complete reconstruction of William Penn's country estate.

Uniontown
Fort Necessity National Battlefield Site—marks place where French and Indian War began.

Valley Forge
State historical park commemorates Washington's headquarters and heroic encampment of 1777–78.

FOR FURTHER READING

Anyone who enjoyed *The Colony of Pennsylvania* may also be interested in the following:

Carpenter, Allan. *Enchantment of Pennsylvania.* Chicago: Childrens Press, 1966.

Foster, Genevieve. *The World of William Penn.* New York: Scribners, 1973.

Haughey, Betty E. *William Penn: American Pioneer.* New York: G. P. Putnam's, 1968.

Syme, Ronald. *William Penn: Founder of Pennsylvania.* New York: Morrow, 1966.

Wallace, Paul. *Pennsylvania.* New York: Harper & Row, 1966.

Colony books published by Franklin Watts:

Alderman, Clifford. *The Colony of Connecticut,* 1975.
Dickinson, Alice. *The Colony of Massachusetts,* 1975.
Goodnough, David. *The Colony of New York,* 1973.
Gurney, Gene and Clare. *The Colony of Maryland,* 1972.
Lacy, Dan. *The Colony of Virginia,* 1973.
Lengyel, Emil. *The Colony of New Hampshire,* 1975.
_____ *The Colony of Pennsylvania,* 1974.
Naden, Corinne J. *The Colony of New Jersey,* 1974.
Vaughan, Harold Cecil. *The Colony of Georgia,* 1975.
Webb, Robert N. *The Colony of Rhode Island,* 1972.

To be published:

Lacy, Dan. *The Colony of North Carolina.*
Lyman, Nanci A. *The Colony of Delaware.*
_____ *The Colony of South Carolina.*

INDEX

Adams, John, 68
Allegheny River, 29
Amen, Jacob. *See* Amish Church.
American Philosophical Society, 62
American Revolution, 26, 47, 58, 62–71, 72–75
American Weekly Mercury, 41
Amish Church, 19, 35
Anglican Church, 20
Articles of Confederation, 73
Assembly, 30, 33, 57, 58, 64

Bartram, John, 41
Bartram, William, 41
Berkeley, John, 20, 27, 29
Bonhomme Richard, 68
Boston Tea Party, 67
Boundaries of Pennsylvania, 3, 4, 26

Brandywine, battle of, 72
Brulé, Étienne, 4, 5
Byllynge, Edward, 20

Callowhill, Hannah, 57
Carteret, George, 20, 27, 29
Champlain, Samuel, 4
Charles I, 21, 22
Charles II, 11, 17, 20, 21, 22, 24, 30, 56
Chesapeake Bay, 5
Columbus, Christopher, 7
Commonwealths in United States, 3
Common Sense (Paine), 67
Concessions and Agreements of West New Jersey, 21
Constitution, Pennsylvania, 30, 32
Constitution, United States, 1

Constitutional Convention, 68, 71, 73, 75
Cromwell, Oliver, 21

Deane, Silas, 68
Declaration of Independence, 1, 47, 68, 75
Delaware River, 3, 8, 29, 30, 35, 39
Dickinson, John, 65
Dixon, Jeremiah. *See* Mason and Dixon Line.
Dunkards, 35

Education, 33, 62, 64
Essay Towards the Present and Future Peace of Europe (Penn), 57
Explorers, 4, 5, 6–11

Farming, 44, 45
Fenwick, John, 20
First Continental Congress, 67
Fort Christina, 8
Fort Duquesne, 54
Fox, George, 14
Franklin, Benjamin, 41, 62–71, 73
French and Indian War, 54, 64
Friends, Society of, 14

Geography, 27–30
George III, 53, 64, 67
Germantown, 36, 44, 73
Government, Colonial, 33. *See also* Assembly.
Great Britain, trouble with colonies, 56–61
Gwynn, Nell, 17

Harrisburg, 3
Henry VIII, 13
Holme, Thomas, 39, 40
Holy experiment (Penn), 21, 61, 75
Howe, William, 72
Hudson Bay Company, 22
Hudson, Henry, 7
Hutter, Jacob, 19–20
Hutterian Brethren. *See* Hutter, Jacob.

Indians, 4, 5, 8, 30, 48–55
Industry, 41
Intolerable Acts, 67

James I, 19
James II, 11, 12, 13, 20, 22, 30, 56
Jamestown colony, 8
Jay, John, 68
Junto, 62

Keystone State. *See* Pennsylvania, nickname.

Lee, Arthur, 68
Lehigh River, 29
Lenni Lenape. *See* Indians.
Liberty Bell, 45, 47
Logan, James, 57, 58
London Board of Trade, 57

Markham, William, 39
Maryland colony, 3
Mason, Charles. *See* Mason and Dixon Line.

Mason and Dixon Line, 3, 26
Mennonites, 19, 35
Minuit, Peter, 7, 8
Monongahela River, 29

New Jersey colony, 3, 4, 20, 27
New York colony, 3, 4, 57
New Netherland, 8, 11
No Cross, No Crown (Penn), 16

Ohio River, 29
Oxenstierna, Axel, 7

Paine, Thomas, 67
Pastorius, Francis Daniel, 35, 36
Penn, Admiral William, 3, 12, 24
Penn, John, 58
Penn, Richard, 61
Penn, Thomas, 58
Penn, William, 29, 30, 33, 35, 56–61, 62, 75
    early history, 12–26
    education, 13
    and the holy experiment, 21
    and Indians, 48–55
    marriages, 20, 57, 58, 61
    and Philadelphia, 39–47
    in New Jersey, 21
    religion. *See* Quakers.
    writings, 16, 57
    founds Pa., 22–26
Pennsylvania
    founding of, 22–26
    motto, 1, 75
    nickname, 1
    statehood, 75

Pennsylvania Dutch, 35, 44, 45
Philadelphia, 1, 33, 35, 36, 39–47, 62, 64, 75. *See also* American Revolution.
Physick, Philip Syng, 44
Plymouth colony, 8
Plymouth Company, 22
Poor Richard's Almanack (Franklin), 62
Puritans, 14, 41

Quakers, 14, 16, 17, 19–21, 33, 38, 40, 41, 44, 48–55, 57, 58, 64

Religious intolerance in England, 13, 56, 57. *See also* Quakers.
Resources, 27, 29, 30
River Brethren, 35
Rush, Benjamin, 44

Sandy Foundation Shaken, The (Penn), 16
Schuykill River, 29, 39
Second Continental Congress, 67
Settlers in Pennsylvania, 35
Ship travel to America, 36
Simons, Meno. *See* Mennonites.
Slavery, 44
Springett, Gulielma Maria, 20
Stamp Act, 65
Stuyvesant, Peter, 8
Susquehanna River, 5, 29

Thomas, Gabriel, 40
Townshend Acts, 65, 67
Truth Exalted (Penn), 16

United Zion Children, 35

Valley Forge, 73
Vaughan, John, 19
Virginia Company, 22

Washington, George, 54, 71. *See also* American Revolution.
William and Mary, 56, 58

York, Duke of. *See* James II.

Emil Lengyel is the author of a number of books for Franklin Watts. He began his writing career on the staff of *The Norristown (Pa.) Times-Herald,* and continued it on *The New York Times.* He now teaches at Fairleigh Dickinson University in New Jersey and makes his home in New York City.